Backyard Birds

Jonathan P. Latimer
Karen Stray Nolting

Illustrations by Roger Tory Peterson

Foreword by Virginia Marie Peterson

Houghton Mifflin Company
Boston

FOREWORD

My husband, Roger Tory Peterson, traced his interest in nature back to an encounter he had with an exhausted flicker when he was only 11 years old. When he found what he thought was a dead bird in a bundle of brown feathers, he touched it and the bird suddenly exploded into life, showing its golden feathers. Roger said it was "like resurrection." That experience was "the crucial moment" that started Roger on a lifelong journey with nature. He combined his passion for nature with his talent as an artist to create a series of field guides and paintings that changed the way people experience the natural world. Roger often spoke of an even larger goal, however. He believed that an understanding of the natural world would lead people — especially young people — to a recognition of "the interconnnectedness of things all over the world." The Peterson Field Guides for Young Naturalists are a continuation of Roger's interest in educating and inspiring young people to see that "life itself is important — not just our-selves, but all life." **—Virginia Marie Peterson**

Copyright © 1999 by Houghton Mifflin Company

Foreword copyright © 1999 by Virginia Marie Peterson

All illustrations from *A Field Guide to the Birds* copyright © 1980 by Roger Tory Peterson and *A Field Guide to Western Birds* copyright © 1990 by Roger Tory Peterson.

Special thanks to Dick Walton for his expert advice.

Library of Congress Cataloging-in-Publication Data

Latimer, Jonathan P.

Backyard birds / Jonathan P. Latimer & Karen Stray Nolting ; illustrations by Roger Tory Peterson ; foreword by Virginia Marie Peterson. p. cm. — (Peterson field guides for young naturalists)

Summary : Describes the physical characteristics, behavior, voices, and habitats of a variety of common birds, arranged by their color. Includes Peterson System of identifying birds by their unique markings.

ISBN 0-395-95210-7 (cl). — ISBN 0-395-92276-3 (pbk.)

1. Birds — Juvenile literature. 2. Birds — Identification — Juvenile literature. [1. Birds.] I. Nolting, Karen Stray. II. Peterson, Roger Tory, 1908–1996, ill. III. Title. IV. Series.

QL676.2.L37 1999   598 — dc21   98-35509 CIP AC

Photo Credits

American Robin: Art Biale; Northern Cardinal: Isidor Jeklin; House Finch: Ted Tauceglia; Blue Jay: Isidor Jeklin; American Goldfinch: L. Page Brown; Eastern Meadowlark: W. A. Paff; Ruby-throated Hummingbird: Mike Hopiak; House Sparrow: Lang Elliott; House Wren: O. S. Pettingill; Mourning Dove: Mike Hopiak; American Crow: Alan Cruickshank; Red-winged Blackbird: O. S. Pettingill; Brown-headed Cowbird: Bob Schmitz; European Starling: Bob Schmitz; Downy Woodpecker: Bill Marchel; Black-capped Chickadee: Isidor Jeklin; White-breasted Nuthatch: Bill Duyck; Rufous-sided Towhee: Stan Smith; Rock Dove: Christopher Crowley; Northern Mockingbird: J. R. Woodward.

Book design by Lisa Diercks. Typeset in Mrs Eaves and Base 9 from Emigre

Manufactured in the United States of America

WOZ 10 9 8 7 6 5 4

CONTENTS

HOW TO WATCH BIRDS

Learning how to watch birds can lead to a lifetime of fun. You can do it just about anywhere — when hiking with your family or friends, riding your bike, or just hanging out in your backyard.

This book will help you recognize some of the birds you are likely to see where you live. It uses illustrations by the man who revolutionized bird identification, Roger Tory Peterson. He invented a simple system of drawings and pointers (now known as the "Peterson System") that call attention to the unique marks on each kind of bird. This book introduces the Peterson System to beginners and young birders. It can help you answer the most important question of all: *What kind of bird is that?*

What Kind of Bird Is That?

Figuring out what kind of bird you've seen is like solving a mystery. You gather clues, and eventually you can find the answer. Sometimes you need only one or two clues. Other times you need more. Solving the mystery is a challenge, but it is also a lot of fun. Try not to get frustrated. You'll get better with practice. Here are some questions you can ask when trying to identify an unknown bird.

What Color Is the Bird? Color is one of the first things you notice when you see a bird. That is why this book is arranged by color. But color alone is not always enough. While there are only a few birds that are blue or red, there are many that are brown or black or white. And there are some, such as pigeons, that can be many different colors.

Does It Have Any Field Marks? Birds have marks, such as spots or stripes, that will help you identify them. For example, a cowbird has brown feathers on its head. A robin has red feathers on its chest. These are called field marks. Field marks can be found on a bird's head, wings, body, or tail. They can help you tell similar birds apart.

How Big Is the Bird? Size is another quick clue to identifying a bird. Is it larger than a sparrow? Is it smaller than a pigeon? The size of the bird will help you rule out some choices and concentrate on others.

What Is the Bird's Shape? The shape of a bird can also help you identify it, even when you can't see its color. Is the bird slender or plump? Does it have a long neck or long legs? What shape is its bill or tail?

Where Did You See the Bird? It is easy to understand that you are more likely to find some birds in certain places. Ducks and geese are commonly found near lakes or rivers, and seagulls are usually found at the seashore. But birds can fly anywhere. You may find ducks or geese a long way from water. Or you may see seagulls far inland. So keep your eyes open. An unexpected bird can turn up wherever you are.

All of the birds in this book can be found in most of the United States and Canada.

Migration
In the spring many birds migrate north to their nesting sites. In the fall they move south to warmer areas where there is more food. Even tiny hummingbirds migrate hundreds of miles. This means that unusual birds may pass through your area during these seasons.

What Is the Bird Doing? As you watch birds you may notice that they behave in certain ways. Some of these behaviors are good clues to the bird's identity. If you see a small bird climbing *down* a tree trunk, it is probably a nuthatch. If you hear a bird drumming on a hollow branch, it is probably a woodpecker. As you become more familiar with birds, you will be able to identify some of them by their behavior alone.

What Does It Sound Like? Some birds have calls or songs that can be recognized immediately. The *coo, coo, coo* of a pigeon or the *cheep, cheep* of a sparrow are familiar sounds. Some birds even say their own names. Listen for the *toe-WHEE!* of a towhee or the *jay, jay!* of a jay. But don't be fooled — a mockingbird can imitate the calls of dozens of birds!

ROBIN

You may have been told that the return of the robin is one of the first signs of spring. In fact, some robins do fly south for the winter and return in spring. But others live year-round in many northern states. During winter these robins stay hidden in woods where they can find food.

In spring and summer you can often see robins running or hopping on lawns. They stop and stand upright, looking for insects and earthworms in the grass. It was once thought that robins could hear earthworms moving underground, but it is now known that robins hunt for their prey by sight.

Robins build their nests wherever there are trees or shrubs to nest in and mud for nesting material. Females do most of the nest building, with some help from the males. The nest is made of twigs and mud, and it is shaped like a cup.

Did You Know?
• A pale blue color similar to the color of robins' eggs is sometimes used in paintings and pottery. It is called robin's egg blue.
• The robin was named by early colonists. The bird reminded them of the robin found in England, which is smaller but also has a red breast.
• The robin's official name is the American Robin. It is the state bird of Connecticut, Michigan, and Wisconsin.

Yellow bill

Dark gray back

Colors slightly paler than male's

Speckled breast with rusty-colored background

(Young)

(Female)

Red breast the color of bricks

(Male)

Habitat Robins live in cities, towns, and forests. They hunt for food on lawns, farmland, and open meadows.

Voice Robins sing in the early morning during spring and summer. Their song is a series of short caroling notes that rise and fall in pitch.

Food In spring and summer robins eat mostly insects and earthworms, which they also feed to their young. In fall and winter they eat mostly fruits and berries.

CARDINAL

The brilliant scarlet red male cardinal is sure to get your attention every time. It is the only red bird with a crest of feathers on its head that lives in North America. It has a black patch around its eyes and a thick red bill. The male cardinal is easy to spot as it flashes through trees or across a garden.

The female cardinal is a little harder to see. She is brown or olive-gray, but her wings and crest are edged in red. She also has a thick red bill.

In spring the female cardinal builds a nest in a dense tangle of vines or bushes. While she sits on her eggs, the male may feed her. After the chicks hatch, both parents bring them food.

Did You Know?
- Cardinals can raise and lower their crests whenever they want.
- The cardinal's official name is the Northern Cardinal. It is the state bird of more states than any other bird — Illinois, Indiana, Kentucky, North Carolina, Ohio, Virginia, and West Virginia.

CARDINAL

Triangle-shaped red bill

Black face

Bright red pointed crest

Looks like female but with black bill

Red edge on crest

Red bill

(Female)

(Young)

(Male)

Habitat Cardinals usually live year-round in dense underbrush along the edges of fields or woods, or in parks in towns and villages. During winter you may see flocks of cardinals numbering as many as 60 or 70 birds.

Voice The cardinal's call often sounds like it is saying *what cheer, what cheer,* or *wheat, wheat, wheat,* or *pret-ty, pret-ty, pret-ty.* They also make a short, sharp call that sounds like *chip.*

Food You can see cardinals hopping around on the ground or moving through shrubs or trees looking for food. They eat a wide variety of bugs, including cater-pillars, beetles, grasshoppers, and even slugs. Cardinals also eat fruits and wild seeds. At a bird feeder they will eat sunflower seeds and corn.

HOUSE FINCH

These lively red and brown birds may become the most frequent visitors to your bird feeder. House Finches are social birds and often appear in small groups, although they sometimes gather in large flocks. Males have a red head and chest, but some males look more orange. Their sides are streaked with brown. Females are brown-striped all over.

House Finches are survivors. They are native to the western United States, but in the 1940s House Finches were captured illegally and sold in New York as pets in cages. When government officials discovered this, bird dealers released their House Finches on Long Island. In a few years wild House Finches were found throughout the greater New York City area. Today they have expanded across the entire United States.

Did You Know?

- Male House Finches sometimes perch on high places and sing for long periods.
- House Finches will hang on a hummingbird feeder and drink the sugar water.

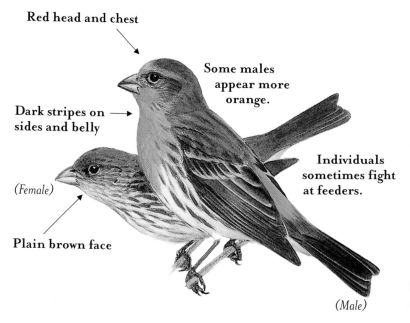

Red head and chest

Some males appear more orange.

Dark stripes on sides and belly

Individuals sometimes fight at feeders.

(Female)

Plain brown face

(Male)

Habitat House Finches have adapted to a wide range of environments. They live in farms, towns, and cities and are familiar backyard birds. They easily adjust to the presence of people.

Voice Listen for the warbling song of the House Finch in your backyard. Males may sing at any time of year. Females sing in spring. Their call sounds like a sweet *cheep.*

Food House Finches seem to be able to eat almost anything. In the country they eat primarily seeds, but in cities they search the streets for crumbs and food scraps. House Finches flock to bird feeders. They will eat a variety of seed, including sunflower and thistle seeds.

JAYS

I t is hard to mistake these loud blue birds for any other bird — they practically shout their name, *jay, jay!* Jays are smart. They are quick to find new sources of food and take advantage of bird feeders. Families of jays travel

together in noisy flocks. The parents will scream loudly and dive-bomb cats, squirrels, and even people who come too close to their young. Several jays will sometimes gang up on an owl, diving at it until they drive it away. This is called "mobbing."

Blue Jays live east of the Rocky Mountains. Larger than a robin, the Blue Jay has a crest of feathers on its head and white spots on its wings and tail.

If you live farther west or in Florida, you may see a Scrub Jay. It behaves much like the Blue Jay, although it tends to be a little more shy around people. It has no crest, and its wings and tail are solid blue.

Did You Know?

• Scrub Jays in Florida have an unusual way of raising their young. A nest is built by a pair of adults, but they may be helped with feeding the young and defending the nest by as many as six "helpers." These helpers are often the pair's offspring from previous years.

Blue Jay

Blue crest

Black necklace

Bold white spots on the wings and tail

Whitish or dull gray chest and belly

Scrub Jay

Brownish tan back

Blue head with no crest

No white spots on wings and tail

Habitat Blue Jays live in woods, towns, and cities. Scrub Jays are found primarily in oak forests. Florida Scrub Jays live in areas with short scrubby oaks that grow in sandy soil.

Voice The most familiar call of the Blue Jay is *jay, jay,* but they also have a call that sounds like *queedle, queedle.* Scrub Jays make a rough, rasping *kwesh, kwesh.* Some jays imitate the calls of other birds, including hawks.

Food Jays eat almost anything, from seeds and fruits to bees, wasps, and beetles. Jays also store acorns in the ground to eat later. At bird feeders they favor sunflower seeds and suet.

GOLDFINCH

If you keep your bird feeder well stocked with thistle or sunflower seeds, you may attract these small yellow birds all year. Male goldfinches look different in summer and winter. In winter they are dull yellow-olive. In spring males become bright yellow with black wings, tail, and cap. In winter females look like males. In spring they are yellow-olive with darker wings marked by two white bars.

Goldfinches live in flocks except during the nesting season. The female builds the nest, usually on the fork of a branch in a hedge or tree. The nest is a compact cup made of plant fibers and spider webs. It is lined with down from thistles or milkweed. These nests are so tightly woven they may even hold water.

The female sits on the eggs and is fed by the male. After the eggs hatch, the male brings her food and she passes it to the young. As the young grow, the male gradually takes over their feeding.

Did You Know?
• Goldfinches fly in an up-and-down pattern like a roller coaster.
• The official name is American Goldfinch, although it is sometimes called a wild canary.
• The goldfinch is the state bird of Iowa, New Jersey, and Washington.

Bright yellow
with black
wings and tail
in summer

Black cap

Yellow-
olive with
black wings

(Male)

(Female)

White bars on wings

In winter
males and females
look alike.

Habitat Goldfinches live in patches
of thistles and weeds. They can be seen on
lawns, along roadsides, and at the edges of woods. They
stay in most parts of North America all year.

Voice Goldfinches often sing as they fly, making a
sound like *ti-dee-di-di* or *per-chik-o-ree* on each dip. Flocks
sometimes sing together as they fly.

Food Goldfinches eat mostly seeds from trees, weeds,
grasses, and flowers, especially daisies. Occasionally they
also eat berries and insects. Goldfinches will come to
feeders for thistle and sunflower seeds.

MEADOWLARKS

Eastern and Western Meadowlarks look alike. They are both chunky birds with a black V on their bright yellow chests. The best way to tell them apart is by their songs. The song of the Eastern Meadowlark is a clear whistle. The song of the Western Meadowlark sounds more like a flute.

When meadowlarks walk, they flick their tails open and shut. When they fly, they beat their wings rapidly several times, then glide, then beat their wings again. You may also be able to see their white tail feathers when they are flying. Meadowlarks often perch atop fence posts in open fields.

Female meadowlarks build their nests in a small hollow in the ground. The nest is shaped like a dome and has a small entrance on one side. It is made by weaving dried grasses and plant stems together.

Did You Know?

- These two meadowlarks look so much alike that Lewis and Clark overlooked the Western Meadowlark on their exploration of the West. Audubon, the great bird illustrator, was the first to recognize the Western Meadowlark as a separate species.
- The Western Meadowlark is the state bird of Kansas, Montana, Nebraska, North Dakota, Oregon, and Wyoming.

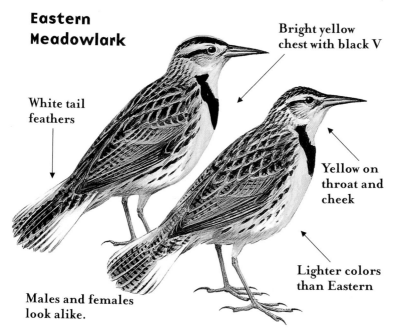

Eastern Meadowlark

Bright yellow chest with black V

White tail feathers

Yellow on throat and cheek

Lighter colors than Eastern

Males and females look alike.

Western Meadowlark

Habitat Meadowlarks can be found all year in fields, meadows, and prairies.

Voice Eastern Meadowlarks have a song with two notes that are drawn out and sometimes repeated. Western Meadowlarks have a 7- to 10-note song that sounds like a flute.

Food Meadowlarks eat many kinds of insects, particularly grasshoppers, crickets, and beetles. They also eat seeds and grain left in farmers' fields after harvest. In spring, flocks sometimes eat corn in fields as it is sprouting.

HUMMINGBIRDS

These fast-moving birds look like little jewels. Their glittering feathers flash bright reds and greens as they dart in and out of the sunlight. Their wings move so fast that they make a humming sound, which is why they are called hummingbirds.

Hummingbirds are spectacular fliers. They can dive or climb at high speed, fly backwards, sideways, or straight up and down. They can start and stop in midair and hover for minutes in front of a flower or a feeder.

Hummingbirds are found only in the Americas. If you live east of the Great Plains, you are most likely to see the Ruby-throated Hummingbird. In the West you may find Black-chinned or Anna's Hummingbirds.

Did You Know?
- Hummingbirds can flap their wings up to 80 times a minute.
- Hummingbirds burn energy very quickly and must eat often. Some eat as often as 15 times in an hour. They even hover in front of spider webs and eat insects trapped there.

HUMMINGBIRDS

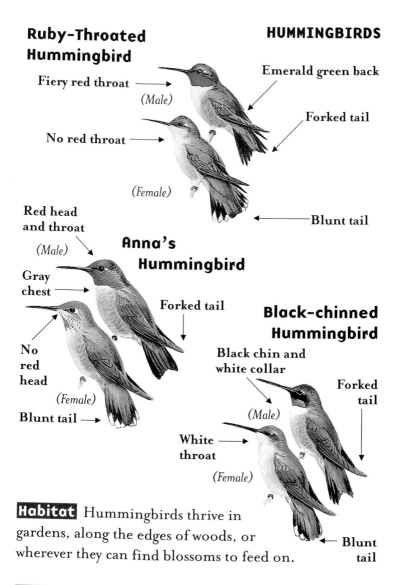

Ruby-Throated Hummingbird

Fiery red throat → *(Male)*

Emerald green back

Forked tail

No red throat → *(Female)*

Blunt tail

Anna's Hummingbird

Red head and throat *(Male)*

Gray chest →

No red head

(Female)

Blunt tail →

Forked tail

Black-chinned Hummingbird

Black chin and white collar *(Male)*

Forked tail

White → throat

(Female)

Blunt tail

Habitat Hummingbirds thrive in gardens, along the edges of woods, or wherever they can find blossoms to feed on.

Voice Hummingbirds sometimes make high squeaks or twitters.

Food Hummingbirds use their long narrow bills to drink nectar from flower blossoms. They also eat tiny insects and small spiders that they find on plants. At feeders they will drink a mixture of sugar and water.

HOUSE SPARROW

It's likely that you've already been approached by one of these friendly little birds. House Sparrows seem almost fearless as they come up to people looking for food scraps.

The success of these birds is astonishing. House Sparrows are native to Europe, Asia, and Africa, but around 1850 a small number were released in Brooklyn, New York. People found them attractive and hoped they would help control insects. The original flock spread quickly. Within 50 years this sparrow could be found throughout the United States and southern Canada.

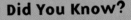

Did You Know?
- The way a House Sparrow looks depends on where it lives in North America. In the rainy areas of the Northwest they are plump and dark. In the dry deserts of Death Valley they are slim and sand-colored.
- The House Sparrow is also known as the English Sparrow.

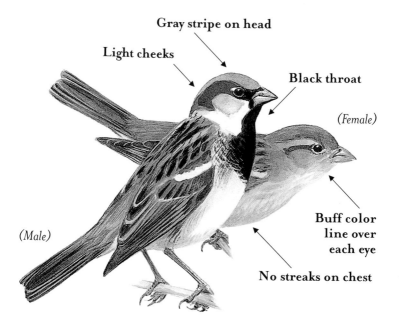

Gray stripe on head

Light cheeks

Black throat

(Female)

(Male)

Buff color line over each eye

No streaks on chest

Habitat House Sparrows have been very successful in living with people. They make themselves at home in cities and farms, but they are rarely found in woods or other undeveloped areas.

Voice Although they are songbirds, House Sparrows have no identifiable song. Their most common call is *cheep, cheep.*

Food House Sparrows eat mainly seeds, but in the warmer months they eat many kinds of bugs. They have even been known to eat insects off the grilles of parked cars. They will also eat scraps and crumbs left by people, and will visit bird feeders.

HOUSE WREN

House Wrens will nest just about anywhere — as long as they can find some sort of hole. The hole can be a natural hollow in a tree, a deserted woodpecker nest, or an opening in a fence or building. Almost any enclosed space will do. House Wrens have been known to nest in flowerpots, old shoes, parked cars, and even in laundry hanging on a clothesline!

The male House Wren collects twigs and uses them to build sample nests in several different holes. He then sings to attract a female. He shows her the sample nests and she selects one. She then completes the nest by lining it with grass, weeds, feathers, and animal hair.

Did You Know?
• The name of the House Wren comes from its habit of nesting close to people's houses.
• House Wrens compete with bluebirds, sparrows, starlings, and other birds for nesting sites.

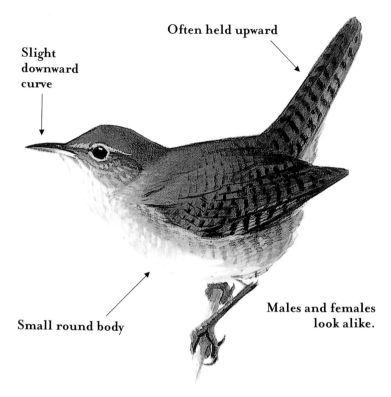

Often held upward

Slight
downward
curve

Small round body

Males and females
look alike.

Habitat House Wrens can be found in open woods and fields and in towns and gardens. They often use nesting boxes people put out for them.

Voice House Wrens have a loud song that is described as gurgling or bubbling. It rises in a musical burst and then falls at the end. They also have a chattering, scolding call.

Food House Wrens eat mostly insects, including beetles, crickets, grasshoppers, moths, and spiders. They will come to a bird feeder for suet.

MOURNING DOVE

Once you hear the sad cooing of a Mourning Dove, you will understand how it got its name. Its call sounds mournful and gloomy and is often heard in the morning or evening. You can easily identify a Mourning Dove at a distance because of its pointed wings and tail.

Mourning Doves are fast fliers. They have been timed at up to 55 miles per hour. In courtship the male flies upward with noisy wingbeats and then glides back to the ground. He puffs out his chest and approaches the female with a bowing movement and a loud cooing song. Once they become a pair, Mourning Doves are known to remain mated for life.

Did You Know?
- Mourning Doves can raise as many as 5 or 6 broods each year, more than any other native bird. Each brood consists of two white eggs.
- To drink, most birds must fill their bill with water and throw their head back to let the water slide down their throat. But Mourning Doves and pigeons can suck water through their bills like a straw.

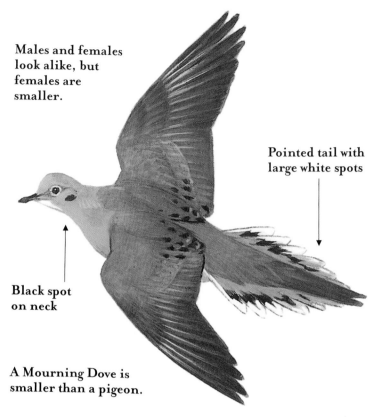

Males and females look alike, but females are smaller.

Pointed tail with large white spots

Black spot on neck

A Mourning Dove is smaller than a pigeon.

Habitat Mourning Doves can be found in almost any open area. Flocks of Mourning Doves can be seen in towns, fields, on farms, and alongside roads.

Voice Mourning Doves have a gentle, sad call that sounds like *coah, cooo, cooo, coo*. If they are startled, their wings make a whistling sound as they fly quickly upward.

Food Mourning Doves usually eat seeds. Although they will sometimes try to feed at a feeder, Mourning Doves usually search below the feeder, eating the seeds that other birds spill.

CROW

Crows are one of the most intelligent birds. They are known to be able to count to 3 or 4. They are also good at solving problems. For example, crows have

learned to break open clams and other shellfish by dropping them on rocks from great heights. Crows can even recognize the difference between a straw-filled scarecrow and a real person.

Crows often travel alone, but in fall and winter they sometimes gather in flocks totaling hundreds of thousands. These flocks eat huge numbers of insects and other pests, but they also can destroy huge amounts of crops. This has made it difficult to decide whether crows are pests as well. But even when they are hunted as pests, crows survive in great numbers because they are so clever and cautious.

Did You Know?
- Crows sometimes steal shiny objects, such as coins or pieces of metal foil, and stash them away.
- Crows and Ravens can be hard to tell apart. Ravens are larger and have a thicker bill and rounder tail.
- The crow's official name is the American Crow. Along the Atlantic coast you may see a Fish Crow, which looks similar to the American Crow.

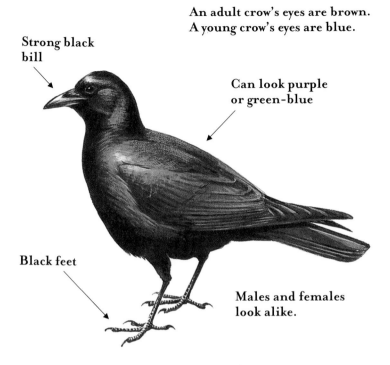

An adult crow's eyes are brown.
A young crow's eyes are blue.

Strong black
bill

Can look purple
or green-blue

Black feet

Males and females
look alike.

Habitat Crows live in open and wooded country, on farm fields, and along rivers or the seashore and in towns and cities. They are often seen standing on the side of the road or flying overhead.

Voice Crows have a familiar *caw, caw* call, but they can also imitate the sounds of dogs, chickens, and even people.

Food Crows usually search for food on the ground. They eat insects, snails, frogs, and other birds. They also eat garbage and scavenge dead animals. Crows are also very fond of corn, which is one reason they are considered pests.

RED-WINGED BLACKBIRD

The arrival of Red-winged Blackbirds is one of the first signs of spring in many places. Flocks of males fly

north in late February or March. Male Red-winged Blackbirds can be seen perched on the highest points in their territories. Females join the males a few weeks later and begin nesting.

Many birds use color as a way of attracting mates and warning off intruders, but only a few can control their display. A familiar example is the tail of the peacock. If you watch Red-winged Blackbirds, you may be able to tell which male owns a nest site and which is an intruder. Owners often display their wing patches while moving around their territory. They will attack intruders, flashing their wing patches and calling loudly. Intruding males usually keep their patches covered and fly away.

After nesting season, Red-winged Blackbirds join cowbirds and grackles in huge flocks. These flocks roost together through winter and can number millions of birds.

Did You Know?
- Young Red-winged Blackbirds climb around on cattails near their nest before they can fly. If they fall into the water, they can swim well enough to make their way back to safety.

RED-WINGED BLACKBIRD

Pointed bill

Mottled brown with red patches

Wing patches concealed

(Young Male)

(Female)

(Male)

Brown with dark stripes on chest

Red and yellow wing patches displayed

Habitat Red-winged Blackbirds nest in marshes and other swampy areas and also in meadows and hay fields. They can be seen looking for food in fields and along the edges of water.

Voice The call of the Red-winged Blackbird sounds like a sharp *check* or a high *tee-err*. Its song is a gurgling *konk-la-ree* or *o-ka-lay*.

Food Red-winged Blackbirds search for food on the ground, often running and hopping along. They eat not only seeds and grain but also insects such as cater-pillars. They will sometimes come to bird feeders for seed or eat bread crumbs scattered on the ground.

BROWN-HEADED COWBIRD

The strangest thing about these birds is the way they raise their young. Cowbirds do not build their own nests. Instead, the female usually removes an egg from

another bird's nest and lays her own in its place. This is called "parasitism." The cowbird is a parasite to more than 200 different kinds of birds.

In many cases, the owners of the nest don't seem to notice the difference between their eggs and the cowbird's. They simply treat the cowbird's egg as their own and raise the cowbird chick. A baby cowbird may grow to twice the size of its foster parents before it leaves the nest.

Some birds do recognize that the cowbird's egg is not theirs. Often they push the egg out of the nest or leave the nest and build a new one. The problem with cowbird parasitism is that it keeps the foster parents from raising their own chicks. In some cases this has threatened the survival of other kinds of birds.

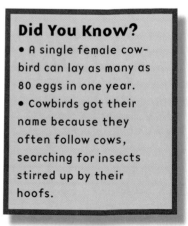

Did You Know?
- A single female cowbird can lay as many as 80 eggs in one year.
- Cowbirds got their name because they often follow cows, searching for insects stirred up by their hoofs.

BROWN-HEADED COWBIRD

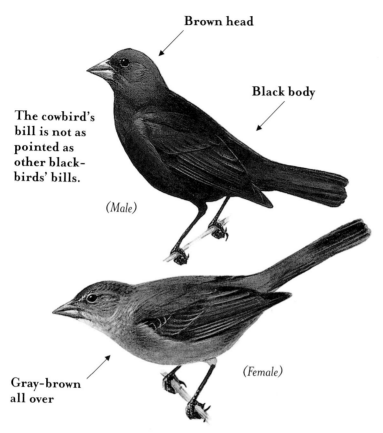

Brown head

Black body

The cowbird's bill is not as pointed as other black-birds' bills.

(Male)

Gray-brown all over

(Female)

Habitat Cowbirds are found on lawns, in fields and barnyards, along rivers and roads, and at the edges of woods. They often flock together with other blackbirds.

Voice In flight cowbirds make a high whistle that sounds like *weee-titi*. They also use a call that sounds like *chuck* or sing a bubbly *glug-glug-gleeee*.

Food Cowbirds eat seeds and grain as well as insects kicked up by moving cattle. Cowbirds also ride on the backs of cows or mules, picking ticks or other insects from their skin.

STARLING

This loud black bird with its long bill and short tail is easy to spot. It lives almost everywhere people do. Tough and aggressive, starlings are chunky birds that look like black triangles when they fly.

Starlings are a recent arrival to North America. In 1890, 60 to 100 starlings were brought from Europe and released in New York City's Central Park to help control insect pests. By 1940 starlings had spread all the way to California and had become pests themselves. They are noisy and messy and nearly impossible to drive away. Hordes of starlings cause serious damage to fruit crops. On the positive side, starlings eat large quantities of insect pests. Today it is estimated that there are as many as 200 million starlings in the United States and Canada.

Did You Know?
- Winter flocks of starlings and other birds have been estimated to be as large as 10 million birds. Attempts to disperse them with chemicals, loudspeakers, gun shots, or by destroying their habitat have been mostly unsuccessful.
- The starling's official name is the European Starling.

Heavily speckled

Dark bill

Gray-brown

Shimmering feathers

Yellow bill

(Young)

Short square tail

(Winter)

(Summer)

Males and females look alike.

Habitat Starlings can be found on farms and in cities and towns. They also live in parks and open fields.

Voice Starlings make many sounds, including whistles and clicks and a harsh, grating *tseeeer* sound. They also imitate other bird calls and even barking dogs or mewing cats.

Food Starlings hunt for a wide variety of insects in grass and on the ground. In fall and winter, flocks of starlings and other birds feed on beetles, grasshoppers, and other insects.

WOODPECKERS

There are two woodpeckers that you can see almost any-where in North America. The smaller one with the shorter bill is the Downy Woodpecker. It is not direct-

ly related to the larger, longer-billed Hairy Wood-pecker, but they look so much alike that even ex-perienced spotters can mix them up.

Woodpeckers use their pointed bills to peck into bark to find food or to dig their nests. They grip the bark with their strong toes and press against the tree with their stiff tail feathers to gain leverage. They use their long sticky tongues to pull food out of the holes they drill.

Both Downy and Hairy Woodpeckers also pound with their bills to attract mates and to warn intruding woodpeckers away. During nesting season males and females will drum on almost any surface that makes noise. They drum on hollow branches, on rain gutters or pipes on houses, and even on metal trash cans.

> **Did You Know?**
> • Woodpeckers can be hard to see because they move to the other side of a tree trunk when people come near.

Downy Woodpecker

White back

Short bill

(Female)

Red patch on back of head

(Male)

The Downy is the smallest woodpecker.

White back

Long bill

Red patch on back of head

(Female)

(Male)

Hairy Woodpecker

Habitat Woodpeckers live in all kinds of forests, river groves, orchards, and shade trees.

Voice The Downy Woodpecker has a sharp note that sounds like *peck!* The Hairy is much louder and sounds more like *pick!* But it is more likely that you will hear the sound of their drumming than the sound of their calls.

Food Woodpeckers eat mostly insects, especially beetles, ants, and caterpillars. They also eat the larvae or eggs of insects they find under tree bark. Woodpeckers will come to feeders for suet.

BLACK-CAPPED CHICKADEE

These little acrobats are a lot of fun to watch. Chickadees spend almost as much time hanging upside down on branches and bird feeders as they do right-side up. Quick-moving and curious, chickadees are among the first birds to appear at a new feeder. Watch them dart in, take a seed, and fly away. They often store seeds in the nooks and crannies of tree bark to eat later.

Chickadees usually stay around all year. A male and female make their nest in a hole in rotten wood or in an old woodpecker hole. The pair digs the hole together. Then the female lines the hole with soft material such as threads, feathers, moss, or hair.

With patience you may be able to teach chickadees to eat seeds out of your hand. Stand very still near a bird feeder where chickadees feed. Hold sunflower seeds in the open palm of your hand so the chickadees can see them as they fly by. It may take a while, but if you are successful, it is worth the effort.

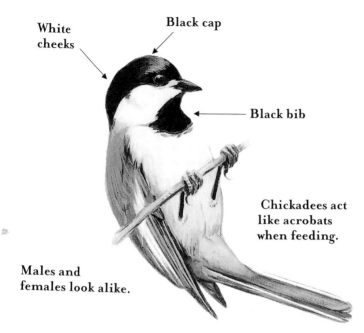

White cheeks

Black cap

Black bib

Chickadees act like acrobats when feeding.

Males and females look alike.

Habitat Look for chickadees in wooded areas or in trees and shrubs near houses.

Voice Chickadees get their name from the call they make. Listen for their cheery-sounding *chick-a-dee-dee-dee* throughout the year.

Food Chickadees eat mostly insects, seeds, and berries. At bird feeders they especially like sunflower seeds and suet.

Did You Know?
- If disturbed on its nest, a female Black-capped Chickadee will hiss like a snake.
- The Black-capped Chickadee is the state bird of Maine and Massachusetts.

TOWHEES

If you hear a rustling of leaves during a walk in the woods, take a careful look. You may find a towhee searching for food. Towhees rummage through the dead leaves on the forest floor looking for insects and seeds. They are more often heard than seen.

If you do see a towhee, watch how it moves. It may make a little jump forward, then scratch backward with both feet at once, shoving the leaves aside. You may also see it hopping backward, raking through the leaves with its bill.

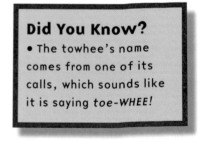

Did You Know?
• The towhee's name comes from one of its calls, which sounds like it is saying *toe-WHEE!*

For a long time the Eastern Towhee and the Spotted Towhee of the West were thought to be a single species called the Rufous-sided Towhee. But recent research has shown that the two species are really separate.

White cheeks

Black cap

Black bib

Chickadees act like acrobats when feeding.

Males and females look alike.

Habitat Look for chickadees in wooded areas or in trees and shrubs near houses.

Voice Chickadees get their name from the call they make. Listen for their cheery-sounding *chick-a-dee-dee-dee* throughout the year.

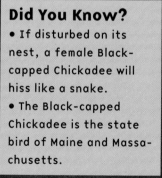

Did You Know?
- If disturbed on its nest, a female Black-capped Chickadee will hiss like a snake.
- The Black-capped Chickadee is the state bird of Maine and Massachusetts.

Food Chickadees eat mostly insects, seeds, and berries. At bird feeders they especially like sunflower seeds and suet.

NUTHATCHES

Most birds climb *up* trees, but nuthatches are different. Nuthatches go down tree trunks headfirst. That is why they are sometimes called "upside-down birds." This behavior helps them find insects in the bark of trees that birds climbing up may have missed.

These small birds have blue-gray backs with lighter-colored breasts. They have large heads, strong bills like a woodpecker, and short, square-cut tails.

Nuthatches often show up together with chickadees and woodpeckers at bird feeders. They seem unafraid of people and may come close to someone standing very still.

The White-breasted Nuthatch has a white face and breast. The Red-breasted Nuthatch has a rusty red breast and is smaller than the White-breasted.

Did You Know?
- Nuthatches have strong toes and claws that grip the bark as they walk up, down, and all around tree trunks and branches. Unlike woodpeckers, they do not use their tails to prop themselves up against trees.
- To open a hard seed, a nuthatch will wedge it into a crevice and pound on it with its bill. This behavior of "hacking" on nuts may be how this family got its name.

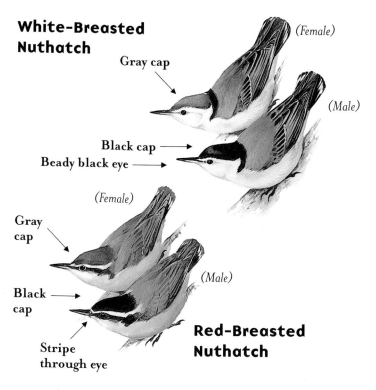

White-Breasted Nuthatch

(Female)

Gray cap

(Male)

Black cap
Beady black eye

(Female)

Gray cap

Black cap

(Male)

Stripe through eye

Red-Breasted Nuthatch

Habitat Nuthatches are found in the woods and forests. In years when cone crops are poor in the North, large numbers of nuthatches may travel south in fall. When there is plenty of food, they stay in their nesting territory through winter.

Voice The call of the White-breasted Nuthatch is a nasal *yank, yank, yank.* Its song is a series of rapid whistles. The song of the Red-breasted is softer and more musical.

Food In summer nuthatches feed mostly on insects and spiders. In winter they eat lots of seeds, which they store in cracks in tree bark. They will come to bird feeders for sunflower seeds and suet.

TOWHEES

If you hear a rustling of leaves during a walk in the woods, take a careful look. You may find a towhee searching for food. Towhees rummage through the dead leaves on the forest floor looking for insects and seeds. They are more often heard than seen.

If you do see a towhee, watch how it moves. It may make a little jump forward, then scratch backward with both feet at once, shoving the leaves aside. You may also see it hopping backward, raking through the leaves with its bill.

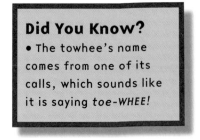

Did You Know?
• The towhee's name comes from one of its calls, which sounds like it is saying *toe-WHEE!*

For a long time the Eastern Towhee and the Spotted Towhee of the West were thought to be a single species called the Rufous-sided Towhee. But recent research has shown that the two species are really separate.

Eastern Towhee

Brown head and back

(Young)

Brown and white streaks →

Black head and back →

Red eyes

Red-orange sides

(Female)

White patches on corners of tail

(Male)

Red-orange sides

Black head and back

(Male)

White spots on wings →

(Young)

Brown and white streaks →

(Female)

Gray-brown

Spotted Towhee

Habitat Towhees live in bushy undergrowth and along the edges of woods.

Voice The towhee's song sounds like *drink-your-teeee* and rises at the end. Their call note is a loud *chewink!* or the sound of their name, *toe-WHEE.*

Food In summer towhees eat mostly ants, beetles, caterpillars, snails, and spiders. In winter they eat seeds, acorns, and berries.

PIGEON

The common city pigeon was the first bird to be tamed by humans. Raised for food and racing for thousands of years, it has also been trained to carry messages. Pigeons are very fast fliers, and their homing ability is legendary. Yet many people now think of them as nuisances.

The official name of the pigeon we see in cities is Rock Dove. They were named this because of their habit of nesting on cliffs and rock faces. Today ledges on tall buildings provide a similar setting that is ideal for nesting.

Did You Know?
- The results of the first Olympic games were carried across ancient Greece by pigeons.
- Pigeons have been clocked flying at speeds of nearly 90 miles per hour.

The pigeon's ability to find its way home over long distances has been carefully studied. On cloudless days they use the sun to locate the right direction. On overcast days pigeons may use the earth's magnetic field to guide them. Once they are near home, they seem to recognize landmarks to find their way.

Chunky body, usually seen walking on the ground

Pigeons can also be white, brown, pink, or many other colors.

White spot

Bright colored patch on neck

Males are usually larger than females, but both have similar markings.

Black wing bars

Habitat Pigeons are found in every city. Look for them in parks and open areas.

Voice Pigeons make a soft cooing sound.

Food Pigeons look for their food by walking around. In the wild, pigeons eat all kinds of grain, seeds, and grasses.

MOCKINGBIRD

Mockingbirds are well known for their ability to imitate the songs of other birds. They have also been heard copying croaking frogs, barking dogs, the notes of a piano, and even the sound of a squeaky wheelbarrow. Males may sit on a high perch and sing all day or all night, especially in the moonlight. They often repeat the same song over and over, sometimes making small changes in it as they sing.

Mockingbirds are very active and curious, moving quickly to check out anything new in the neighborhood. They are almost fearless when defending their nest and young. They will drive away hawks, owls, snakes, cats, dogs, and even humans by diving at them again and again.

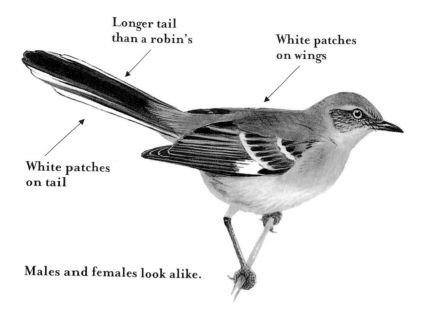

Longer tail
than a robin's

White patches
on wings

White patches
on tail

Males and females look alike.

Habitat Mockingbirds are usually around all year. They are found in towns, on farms, and along roadsides.

Did You Know?
• One mockingbird was heard imitating the calls of 32 different birds in just 10 minutes.
• The mockingbird's official name is the Northern Mockingbird. Five states have chosen it as their state bird. They are Arkansas, Florida, Mississippi, Tennessee, and Texas.

Voice Mockingbirds make a wide variety of sounds, but you can easily recognize their harsh call, which sounds like *tchack* or *chair*.

Food During spring and summer mockingbirds hunt for insects while walking or running on the ground. In fall and winter they eat mostly berries and other fruit.